Think Big to find Success

Think Big to find Success

Learning to break free of thoughts that are holding you back

JOSIE BAXTER.

Copyright © Josie Baxter 2018

All rights reserved world wide

No part of 'Think Big to find success' may be reproduced or stored by any means without the express permission of Josie Baxter

Whilst reasonable care is taken to ensure the accuracy of the information in this publication, no responsibility can be accepted for the consequences of any actions based on any opinions, information or advice found in the publication.

ISBN-13: 978-1717133960

Contents

Introduction 9
What does success mean? 15
    What is success? 17
Define success 20
    What is your 'why'? 20
    What is your need? 24
    Take the next step. 26
Stop Thinking Small 31
    Thinking small. 33
    You Keep Ideas to Yourself 35
    You don't Trust Others 36
    You Dislike Your Competition 39
    Just Getting By 42
    The Future is bleak 44
    You're Risk Averse 46
    You Feel Entitled 47
    You Act in Fear 49
    You Have No Self-Confidence 51
    Your 'small' thinking 54

- Start Thinking Big 59
  - You Share Knowledge 59
  - You Build Relationships 62
  - You Love Your Competition.......................... 64
  - You Love giving.. 66
  - You're Optimistic.. 67
  - You Take Risks 69
  - You Are Grateful... 71
  - You are Confident 73
- How to Succeed 77
  - Personal Life 80
  - Your Career 84
  - Setting goals 87
  - Your relationships.. 88
  - Money... 92
  - Life Purpose... 95
  - Reaching Prosperity....................................... 99
- Learn how to Achieve your goals 107
  - Have Action steps 108
  - Hold yourself accountable.......................... 109
  - Learn self-discipline.................................... 110

Talk to yourself 111
The Categories Of Life 115
Momentum 118
Failure is Your Best Friend 120
The Reward System 123
How to Train Your Brain 126
The Art of Visualizing 131
Meditate 134
Create Success Habits 137
And finally 140

Introduction

The whole concept of thinking big is probably totally alien to you.

If it wasn't you wouldn't have picked up this book.

Most people tend to hold themselves back from happiness by expecting that they will never really find it.

Most of us are programmed by our families, our friends, our peers, the media - by life in general - to think small or at least to keep thinking limited.

We learn not to set our goals too high, to think that our dreams are just that, out of reach dreams.

In fact you even call them your wildest dreams, which tags them immediately as being impossible, out of reach and something that other people will achieve in life, not you.

But why?

Why do we limit ourselves and our success before we even start a new project?

And why do we so often tie our idea of happiness to someone else?

To meeting the right man, to finding the right relationship, to our children and their success.

Of course, this is all very important and often creates a wonderfully happy and successful life, but it doesn't always and in the meantime you have given away your power.

The other idea of what success and happiness is always seems to be about money.

If I were rich, I would be happy.

More money means more success.

I should have been born rich!

Bit that's very narrow thinking and it can hold you back by putting blocks in place in your life.

Okay, some people start life with the money - but not all do, and many of those who do, still fail spectacularly.

So it's not a matter of being born with a silver spoon.

Some people have a better education, but then some of our greatest entrepreneurs, our greatest success stories have hardly traditional any education at all, having left school at 16 or 18 without a string of exam successes to their name.

So it's not that.

Some of the most amazing success stories you will read about have very humble beginnings.

People who arrive in a country with next to nothing and create a multinational business.

People who have been written off at school as never having a chance of making anything of themselves become huge stars.

But then there are people who will never be the star of the show, who will never reach the rich list, who will never become famous

- and will never want any of that –

but they will be the happiest people you will ever find.

We might have been programmed in this material world to think that success equals fame and fortune, but it doesn't.

Success in life is about being happy in life.

Being contented enough to be able to deal with the ups and downs of any normal life.

Happy with their families, happy with where they live, happy with their lifestyle - achieving a success in life beyond their wildest dreams.

So in this book we will look at what success really means to you, how to break the barriers

Think Big

that are holding you back and how you can learn to aim for your personal dream and the steps you can take to reach it.

After all when you are happy and know what your success is, you will be able to take those you love with you on your journey.

Think Big

Think Success

Think Big

What does success mean?

So what do you imagine when you think of success?

Do you picture having millions in the bank, living in a mansion, having a fancy car outside the door and luxury holidays on tap?

And who is at the provides these riches.

Have you created your own wealth, have you created the riches as a family or a couple, or is your dream to marry into it.

That's what success means to a lot of people in their imagination.

And to a lot of women the ideal picture of a successful life is one of being the partner of the rich and famous man.

Their picture of what they will be is when they are rich and possibly famous. When they win the lottery. When they become a social media star. When they marry someone fabulously rich.

But is that really success?

Does that really make people happy?

If they were the things that you needed for a successful life we wouldn't read stories of the rich and famous entering rehab or having a seemingly endless stream of weddings and divorces.

We are bombarded in the media and even more so online, with stories of people who've gone from rags to riches, who are able to use their new Internet skills to work two hours a week and deliver a luxury lifestyle.

Unfortunately, the stories feed a sense of dissatisfaction and failure in the vast majority of us, and we're basing that on stories that are probably not even true. We're basing it on the photoshopped, edited perfection of social media. It's no more true that the fairy tales we read as children

The only thing the stories really do is rob you of your confidence, your hope, your positive attitude and quite often your money as you invest your hard earned cash and time and dreams into schemes that are only designed to make the sellers rich and magic products that fail to live up to you expectations.

Think Big

It's time to step back and think about what success really is, and what success really means to you.

What is success?

Success is a very personal matter.

There's no doubt that there are some people for whom success means becoming rich.

And I'm sure some of them are very happy being very rich, but then there are lots of people that are very happy without being very rich and lots of people who are rich and are extremely unhappy.

If you look on those news sites you can also find stories from successful entrepreneurs and business people who have left the corporate world and followed their dream instead and are blissfully happy growing organic vegetables and being self-sufficient or selling ice cream somewhere in the Caribbean.

They might have ditched their life of riches and privilege, but they too are abundantly happy and successful, in many cases happier than they were in their previous life.

So success is a very personal matter.

For some it is lots of money, for others it's doing something very fulfilling, and for some people it's the freedom of living the life you dream of.

The really important thing is to decide what success is to you.

What really is a life beyond your wildest dreams?

This can sometimes be quite a difficult thing to work out, but it's vitally important if you are ever to achieve true happiness and fulfilment.

You might have grown up in a family where it was expected that you would become a doctor, or a lawyer, or an accountant or go into the family business or have the big wedding and the 2.4 children and stay at home baking cookies.

Your idea of success has always been focused on these expectations.

For instance, if you were expected to go into the field of medicine.

You were expected to do well, whether that meant having your own practice, becoming a top surgeon or dedicating your life to a career as a nurse.

You became so indoctrinated with this plan for you and your path in life, that you have taken it on board as your own dream.

But is it?

Or was your dream always something you kept quiet at the back of your mind, some part of you that really want to grow your own fruit and vegetables and bottle them and create preserves that you could sell at the local market.

You have to follow your own happy to reach genuine success in life.

So to truly be successful, to think big and aim for your dreams, you first of all need to work out what your dreams actually are, otherwise you are spending a lifetime getting in your own way.

Define success

Let's start this process with defining your own idea of what success means to you.

Here are a few tips on how to define what success is to you and only you:

What is your 'why'?

So you have this idea of what success means to you.

When you sit somewhere quiet, close your eyes and breathe deeply, you can see what your perfect future is – your daydream.

But take this a step further and ask yourself some important questions, the first of which is - why?

Why do you want to achieve this dream?

Think Big

Have you ever really thought about this or have you just been following something pre-programmed into you?

Are you following something that you think is your dream because you grew up with that message.

Is it the big white wedding, the show-house and the 2.4 children?

Is it the career path that a modern woman should pursue?

Is it chasing the glamorous, perfect body that you think you should have in order to be beautiful?

Are these your dreams or just the dreams you think you should have.

It's time to really look at who you are and what you want out of life, so it's time to take a long hard look at your idea of success.

This is a very important part of the process, and it can be quite a difficult one. You may be overturning things that you have believed for a lifetime and that can be uncomfortable, but if you don't understand why something is important to you then you will never have any chance of living the life you really want.

So give yourself time at this stage.

Don't rush it, you don't need to decide in the next five minutes, this can literally be a life changing process and it deserves - and you deserve - investing the time to get it right.

It might be a stage you come back to after you have read further in this book, because it may take a little more soul-searching before you understand how truly important this part is.

Once you've found your why, you should have a better idea of whether this really is your dream, or if your own hopes and wishes have been drowned out by what you think is expected of you.

If this is truly your dream, why is it your dream?

What you expect to get out of it?

How do you expect to feel once you have achieved that goal?

What do you think you will do with your success and with life after you have achieved that goal?

As I said, this is a very important stage of the whole process so it is worth taking the time and the effort to take this stage seriously.

You need to be prepared to dig deeply into yourself, you need to be prepared to think seriously, to meditate so that you can discover what genuinely is your true calling, your passion and purpose in life.

Everyone has one and it doesn't matter what it is, as long as it deeply and genuinely matters to you.

At some point everyone asks themselves,
What am I doing?
Is there something more than this?
Who am I?

There are as many answers to this question as there are people in the world and you need to find your answer.

Not what you think your answer is, not what you think your answer should be, but your real answer.

The earlier you can do this the better because otherwise you may find yourself reaching retirement and wondering what it was all about.

Personally, I discovered what I really want to be able to do is help other people to solve their own problems, I love to be able to spread knowledge to as many people as I can reach, to give them the tools to improve their own lives. That is what gives me satisfaction and makes me happy at the end of the day.

I also love the fact that I am able to work at home, at my own pace, creating balance between life and work and of course been able to do work that I love.

You may love being able to work with nature.

Your passion might be teaching children, showing them how to get the most out of life.

You may love the cut and thrust of the corporate world, or the challenge of creating your own enterprise.

Your true happy place might be when you are being creative with either paints or fabrics or camera or food.

It doesn't matter what your personal happy is, what your personal picture of success is, as long as it is yours.

That is the very first stage of creating a successful life.

What is your need?

Once you have worked out what is your why, you will be able to see what your core need or desire is.

This is a natural progression from the why.

Once you decide why you want to do a particular thing in life, and equally importantly why you don't want to do something, you will be able to see what you need.

All of us have a burning desire or need inside us if we only give it a chance to show itself.

Most of us stamp on this desire so hard that it fades to a tiny little light flickering deep inside us that we can't see any more.

Think Big

There are many reasons why we choose to ignore our deep desires.

- You might think it's impractical.
- You might think you will never succeed.
- You might think you will disappoint others.
- You might think it doesn't make financial sense.
- You might think it's the kind of thing that other people do.

But once you give it some air, some hope, it will rekindle and you will be able to see what you deeply and truly desire to achieve in life.

And once you've rediscovered what your dreams actually are, you will be able to plot a path towards them.

You might have a driving need to be your own boss, to be the captain of your own ship, a desire that you have firmly stomped on in the belief that it's not possible for you.

You might realise that your deepest held wish is to be able to help others, a passionate desire to show others how they can improve their own lives.

You might admit to yourself that your real passion is to create a loving and supportive home life for your family, rather than working a minimum wage and spending it all on childcare and ready meals because that's what's expected of the modern woman.

You will only ever find true success and happiness when you follow your own inner desires rather than doing what you think is expected of you.

Take the next step.

Once you know what your why is and what your need is you will be able to see what your goal is.

And that's great, that's probably clearer than you've ever been, but now you need to know what your path to that goal is.

You need to know what steps you will have to take to get you there.

This is the stage at which you have to leave the comfort of thinking and step into the world of planning.

Up until this point it has all been theoretical.

It might have been pleasant, like a wonderful daydream, living in a dream world where anything and everything is possible.

It might also of being quite uncomfortable, even unpleasant to realise how far from the true you your life has drifted.

But so far it has all been internal.

In order to reach the next stage, you have to be able to step out into the world of action.

The world of how.

This is where the real changes will take place. This is where you will be able to turn daydreams into a real plan. And that is extremely important.

As the old saying goes if you fail to plan, you plan to fail.

So in the rest of this book, we will be looking at how to put the plan into action so that you can achieve that success that you want.

Think Big

Think Big

Small thinking

Think Big

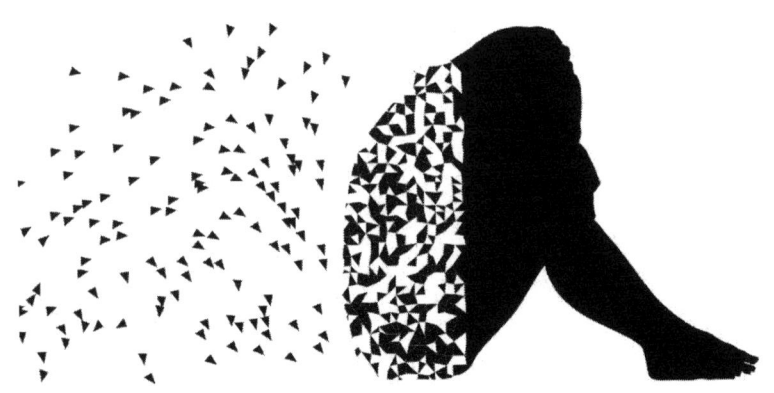

Stop Thinking Small

There are basically two ways of thinking in this world, two types of people.

There are the people who think big, who think that everything is achievable, that they can succeed, they can be happy, they can get where they're planning to be.

Then there's the majority of people.

The people who think small.

Sometimes this can be called scarcity thinking and it's basically an idea that there isn't enough.
- Not enough to go around,
- Not enough for you to have part of it
- Not enough for you to be successful and happy.

And of course, this small thinking really isn't your fault.

Think Big

Most people have been taught by the world around them since childhood that there isn't enough.

There isn't enough money, there isn't enough time, there aren't enough chances.

Abundance, success, happiness always belongs to someone else and there isn't enough to go around.

It's the idea that keeps people down. Keeps them in a boring 9-5 job. Keeps them in a cramped apartment in a dissatisfied life.

Then there are the people who think big, sometimes referred to as abundance thinking.

They are the people who believe that there is always more than enough for anyone and everyone if only we allow ourselves to accept that.

The word can't, just doesn't figure in their vocabulary. They might not be ready to do a specific thing at a specific time, but they never consider that they can't do it.

It just never occurs to them that the cake might not be big enough for them to have a slice - and for everybody else to have a slice as well. They want to share their success and happiness.

First of all, let's take a closer look at scarcity thinking, after all you have to understand the problem before you can work on the solution.

Thinking small.

When you think small you will automatically believe that there will never be enough no matter how hard you work.

This means that you behave as if you are always in competition with the rest of the world because you have to protect your own share of the limited resources.

This means that you can hoard things, whether that is actual things, money or ideas and your skills.

You hold things close to yourselves because you think they are in a limited supply which means that you cannot afford to share them and help others, they might take your supply and leave you without.

That might sound very strange, and your reaction might be because you don't feel like that.

But think about it.

Maybe you treat the rest of the world as if they are in competition with you.

Maybe you are constantly watching your back at work because you expect others to take your ideas, expect others to take the promotion that you should get, you might even live life being terrified of being replaced, whether that is at work or even in your own personal life.

There is a horrible saying at the moment:

'life's crap then you die'.

That is such a negative attitude to live with, but it's an attitude that seems to have become almost the norm for many people.

If you carry this idea with you, if you live with a chip on your shoulder, if you live in terror of being replaced and undermined, how are you ever going to be happy?

If you sink yourself into the mindset that times are tough and getting tougher, that there's no such thing as true love, that you really can't trust anyone other than yourself, the change is dangerous and risk is something to be feared, you are creating your own nightmare.

Negativity can sap your energy, your hope and your health, and it becomes a self fulfilling prophesy.

Most people aren't so completely negative (although some folk are), but you might recognise some of those traits in yourself even if they only surface sometimes when you are feeling particularly bleak. But they are sapping your energy and they are beliefs that are limiting you, so let's look at them individually.

Think Big

You Keep Ideas to Yourself

You have a great idea, and it is your idea, and it is valuable, so you can't possibly share it with someone else who will steal it from you.

What exactly is the good of an idea that you don't share with the rest of the world?

That's like being a miser who keeps his money under the mattress.

Money is only actually worth something once it is spread around. While it's under the mattress it's only bits of paper, bits of paper that can be burnt, or damaged, or devalued - it's really worthless.

But money that you earn and take to the store and spend, will then spread to the people working in the store, the people who work in the company that produces the goods for the store, the people who work in the companies or on the farms that produce the raw materials for the goods, who will then take their wages and go out for a nice meal in the restaurant that you work for, which pays your wages.

Money only really works when it's being spread around.

Ideas are the same.

There is no point hoarding an idea to yourself in case someone else steals it, because it might be 100% safe but isn't doing you any good either.

So not only are you stopping somebody else benefiting from your idea, you are even stopping yourself benefiting from it.

Some people write a book, but they are then so terrified that someone else might copy it and steal their work that they never share it with anybody. What good is a book that nobody reads? It's a simple answer - it's absolutely no good at all except as a doorstop.

So don't hoard your ideas, share them, spread them, work with other people to mingle your ideas with their ideas and in the process you will probably create something that is better than the sum of its parts.

You don't Trust Others

One of the problems with thinking small is in relationships.

If you feel there isn't enough to go around, that you are always having to protect yourself and that makes it extremely hard to be able to trust anyone else.

That means it can be difficult trusting people at work, whether it's the people you work with or your bosses.

It can be difficult trusting friends, after all surely they are looking out for themselves and their own interests.

It means you can feel suspicious when people are nice to you. What are they up to, what do they want?

And of course it can make it very difficult to form any deep and meaningful personal relationship. How can you create a successful long-term relationship if you don't trust someone?

Trusting people can be very difficult if you read the newspapers and particularly some of the stories online and follow social media.

There are mornings when you open the paper and all you see is bad, negative news.

But think about it another way.

If murder and violence were actually normal, then it wouldn't be news.

In our modern world, communication is both fast and worldwide, so the latest trouble can be spread into our living rooms from anywhere in the world in minutes.

Our parents and grandparents would never have heard most of the bad news that we are bombarded with, but because news has become a 24-hour business there is a constant demand for a supply of sensational new stories.

Of course crime and violence is terrible for anyone who is suffering it, but the truth is that most of us don't suffer it.

That doesn't mean we have to ignore the plight of those who do - they deserve and need our help.

But for most of us, we don't have to live in constant fear of it happening to us. We don't have to mistrust every person we pass in the street.

If you find it difficult to believe that most people are kind, try this experiment.

Next time you're walking through the store, lift your head up, smile at people, hold the door open or lift an item from a high shelf that someone can't reach. Some people won't take any notice of you, but they are the people that are still having a tough time learning to be open.

You will be surprised at how many people smile back at you, how many people say thank you, how many people hold the door open for you rather than slamming in your face. Most people are nice when you give them a chance. And being nice is very good for reducing stress, so it's good for you as well as everyone else.

You Dislike Your Competition

Automatic dislike of your competitors is small thinking - very small thinking.

You'll see it across the spectrum, where football fans get into fights with their rivals, schools break up into cliques and groups, political enemies attack each other on a personal level, and business competition tries to lobby the government to stop others from competing.

Most of this happens due to having limiting beliefs and scarcity thinking on a mass scale.

Most of us are used to thinking of competition in terms of business and the businesses we deal with, although the problems with thinking negatively about competition and our competitors can hit at any part of life.

So lets look at it from a business perspective.

Of course it's true that everyone can't sell exactly the same thing and expect to earn enough money, companies have to distinguish their products, even if it's only slightly, even if it's only on price.

That's healthy competition.

But it is easier to make sales when the basic product is slightly different or better in some

Think Big

way. That's why there are so many different cosmetic companies, clothing stores and car manufacturers.

Making something a little better or a little different will help competition. But that doesn't mean a company has to destroy their competition by putting them out of business.

In fact in most successful industries, different companies work together.

If you find this difficult to believe consider all the industry events that happen. Travel agents from all over the country will get together to meet and mingle and talk and discuss business.

And this happens across all sorts of industries. Just think about how many big conventions and conferences that are held every week of the year.

When competitors get together in any industry event, the smart people will work hard to meet other smart people who like sharing. They talk together, learn new ideas, and then walk away knowing they can make their offerings better.

Networking events allow people who are in competition with each other, to meet and mingle. They share ideas openly and help each other improve, and somehow, even more people start making more money when it's over. There are no limiting beliefs there.

The same thing works in your personal life.

Think Big

Think of the people you work with as members of a team rather than trying to compete against them constantly Scoring points and protecting your back all the time is not only an uncomfortable way to live it's also unproductive in the long term and certainly not the way to have a happy and successful life.

If you work together the company will do better, which means you all do better.

If you're constantly protecting your own corner you won't be able to successfully collaborate with anyone. Why should anybody be prepared to swap shifts with you, cover your work so you can collect a child from school unexpectedly or get to the dentist, if you are always acting as if it's them or you.

Why compete with your neighbour about the state of your front yard, if you work together you can both have a better result.

Why feel you are in competition with your friends or work colleagues about who has the latest fashion or gets the most 'likes'.

Competition is part of life, and positive competition is a wonderful driving force to help you do better in whatever area you choose to compete.

But automatically disliking or even hating your competition just makes life unnecessarily difficult and holds you back from success.

Just Getting By

A lot of people earn just enough money to get by.

Their financial life is a never ending struggle to keep their head above water.

They managed to pay the rent each month, they keep food on the table and they pay the bills, but it always feels as if there is never quite enough or it's always just enough.

But there will be other people with exactly the same set of circumstances who feel happy and satisfied, who do manage to put a bit away and always feel as if they have enough.

This isn't about how much money actually comes into the house, it's about your attitude to money.

Now I'm not for a moment saying that money can be a problem at times, we've been living in a period of austerity for a long time now, but there are still different ways to tackle the financial challenges in your life.

Think Big

There are people who live in mansions and drive expensive cars who just managed to keep their head above water every month, and are quickly on the brink of disaster if anything goes wrong.

And there are people on minimum wage who live comfortably and happily and always have some put aside for a rainy day.

There are also people who are prepared to do something about getting more or making more of what they got.

The ones with the never enough, often have a problem caused by the way they look at money and how they consider it to be limited.

Some people feel guilty about wanting more money or just about wanting more.

Deep down they have an idea that it is selfish to want more, that it's really not the thing to do, but it's not their place to expect more out of life.

This attitude can mean that they always expect to just get by – whether they get by on burgers and thrift store clothes, or whether they are getting by on champagne and Manolo Blahniks. This means that they can stop themselves from improving their situation, because deep down they expect it to be difficult.

If you constantly feel negative about life, you will never be able to see your way out of the problems, and if you just don't see that there might be a light at the end of the tunnel you have absolutely no chance of finding it.

If you are just getting by right now, congratulations, you are surviving, but it's time to do more than survive.

Once you learn to reverse the limiting, negative thoughts and open yourself up to more positive beliefs you can break through the attitudes that are holding you back, and the most important thing to realise is that there is enough to go round in this world without stealing someone else's share, you just need to allow yourself to find it.

The Future is bleak

Thinking small is linked very closely to being pessimistic.

In particular, many people who think small tend to be very pessimistic about the future.

You know people like this.

I certainly know people like this!

They always think that the end is near.

They think this is the final straw and the world will end, disaster is just around the corner - whether that's in their own lives or on a worldwide scale, the glass is always half empty – if it even holds that much!

They live their whole lives just waiting for the catastrophe that they know is waiting for them.

But even a disaster doesn't always mean the end of the road.

You may lose your job and of course that will be difficult at the time, but you could get a much better one that you find much more satisfying and that you would never have imagined applying for.

It might be the opportunity to take that step that you have always wanted to take but were afraid to do. Afraid of leaving the comfort zone of your steady job and stepping into the unknown.

In the long term, a failure that seems like a catastrophe, might be the best thing that ever happened to you.

A relationship that fails, means that you are open to a new one – and that might be your lifelong relationship.

A chronic illness or serious injury could open up opportunities you never even knew existed - I know this one from personal experience. Getting M.E./CFS (chronic fatigue syndrome) changed my life entirely, but I love where I am now.

Think Big

You're Risk Averse

Risk is a funny thing. There is nothing wrong with being careful about the risks you take with your life, other people's lives, and your money. However, if you're not willing to take any risks you're going to end up a very lonely and with a poor bank balance.

Life is about risk.

Leaving the house each day involves a certain amount of risk, but then again so does staying in the house if you're really determined to find a risk.

Putting your money in the safest bank still has some form of risk, but so does hiding it under the mattress.

Life is a risk. That's what makes it worth living.

So, living the life of your dreams also will require you to take some risks.

They can be and should be educated risks.

Putting everything you own on a horse in the 3.30pm should probably be considered an incredibly stupid risk, but people put everything they own on their belief in a product or business every day. (Although I wouldn't recommend the horse race).

You have to remember that taking no risk at all in life is also a dangerous choice and could be even riskier than taking an educated risk to do something new and different.

The truth is that thinking small can cause you to make choices that are riskier and more dangerous than thinking big because it can freeze you into inaction which will limit your success in life.

When you think big, you can act in big ways without the crippling fear of making a choice.

You Feel Entitled

It's surprising but true that people who think small, often seem to act as if they're entitled to something that someone else has, in fact they think that they deserve it more than the person who has it.

If you realise that you feel that way about something, you should take a step back at this stage.

Maybe you are smarter than someone else, maybe you are more deserving because you're a nice person and they're not.

Maybe you are better at that job and should have got the promotion.

Maybe you feel that you should live in the bigger house, in the nicer neighbourhood.

But the fact is that jealousy, feeling that you're better that others, feeling entitled and that you have been robbed of your rightful success, is never going to help you reach happiness and true success.

There are definitely times when other people have advantages they haven't necessarily earned, but you can only improve your own life by focusing on yourself rather than feeling bitter and twisted.

Jealousy has always existed in human nature and it has always been ugly and vicious, hurting all of those who are affected, including the people who are feeling the jealousy.

Jealousy can ruin people's lives but it can never make anything better.

Unfortunately, although jealousy has always existed, our modern lifestyles and social media have made it a lot more prevalent, and it's made it seem almost normal.

But the thing is, hating someone else because they've made a success of something in their life is never going to help anyone.

No one deserves the success that someone else has. Everyone only deserves the success that they create for themselves.

So if you find yourself feeling jealous, stop.

Take a good look at what they have done and learn lessons from them. How could you use your skills - and everyone has skills - to create your own success.

Use their success as inspiration to improve your own life

The fact that you are scared of taking a risk, the fact that you don't think you're smart enough or have enough knowledge or experience, is not their fault.

They don't deserve your entitled attitude and jealousy.

Instead, use your energy in a positive manner, to do something better for yourself in your own life.

When someone honestly and ethically achieves success, practice being happy for them and use it as encouragement to work on your own success and happiness.

You Act in Fear

Having small and limiting attitude will also make people act out of fear, especially fear of loss or being left behind.

This can be seen very often in buying things or making decisions, and salespeople are very good at using this fear against us if we don't have the confidence to believe in ourselves and our own opinions.

If you make choices on the spur of the moment, or you buy things or own things that you don't really like or want just because someone else did it, or a website tells you that it's trending, you may be acting in fear.

The idea of being left behind, of being the only one that didn't own that particular piece of clothing, of being unfashionable or not following the trend can create a fear that is so strong that it is irresistible.

Bad choices are often made out of fear.

Why shouldn't I spend a thousand dollars on the credit card to buy that handbag that I like, or that a reality star has bought? After all, it or I might not be here tomorrow.

Why not buy that pair of jeans, it's a limited edition I might miss out.

Everybody is investing in that share, or selling off another share, I better do the same, they must know more than me. That's the type of thinking that leads to a stock market bubble or a stock market crash.

Why can't you trust your own opinion instead of simply being a lemming and following everyone else off the cliff.

You can see where this is going.

When you let go of fear and scarcity thinking, you won't be afraid to ignore fashion and listen to your own opinions which can save you money and trouble and mean that you have and do things that you actually like.

You Have No Self-Confidence

Many people who think small tend to lack self-confidence.

In fact that is normally the main problem behind everything.

Their real reason for not doing more is that they really don't think they're good enough. They don't really believe they deserve anything. Their entitled attitude gets to them and they think they're a bad person and don't deserve happiness, money, and their dream life.

It may seem contradictory to feel entitled but at the same time lack confidence but often the two go together.

It's easier to blame other people than to look at yourself. A lack of confidence can be crippling and it's very difficult to live with.

It can affect every part of your life because you don't feel clever enough, pretty enough, popular enough or deserving enough the success.

This lack of confidence might have been instilled over a lifetime of hearing negative messages.

It might have been parents, teachers, school 'friends', people you live with, people you work with, people on social media.

You might have been listening to these negative messages – negative affirmations – all your life, so it's natural that you will believe them but it's time to take battle against them if you really want to improve things.

The way to overcome your lack of confidence and low self esteem is to do things that help you experience self-confidence.

When you take a risk and do something that is out of your comfort zone, the confidence you will gain from successfully completing the task will improve your self-confidence across all areas of life.

That's why something like bungee jumping or white-water rafting can be so life changing. You can be terrified, absolutely terrified of the prospect but even more terrified of what other people will say if you back out.

So you do it.

You face the lesser of two terrors and jump.

And you find that you have survived.

And magically, the terror turns to self-confidence.

You will feel good about yourself and of course this will improve your self-confidence.

It can be even better if you manage to find a way of doing things for others at the same time.

You could try taking part in a charity parachute jump, or feel the pride and success of getting to the end of a marathon.

On a less drastic scale, you could join a knitting club and feel the companionship and success of creating blankets for those in need as part of a group of knitters.

You could take a course to improve your skills or to learn a new hobby. Each success will help build your self-confidence and give you belief in your ability to succeed.

You can also strengthen your self esteem by using positive affirmation messages to help you rewire your brain.

Think Big

Your 'small' thinking.

If you want to break out of the limits you have placed on yourself it is important at this stage to be honest with yourself.

It's not comfortable and I don't want you to play a blame game – that won't help at all.

But you have to be able to see and to accept the thought patterns that you have in your subconscious that are holding you back.

Most of us have some of them in some parts of our lives and if you didn't feel the need for change you wouldn't have picked up this book.

So the first stage of making changes is being realistic and honest with yourself.

If you can't or won't see where the problems are you will never be able to move on from this stage and work on creating a new more successful, happier life for yourself.

It can be helpful to reread this part of the book, this time being kinder to yourself.

It doesn't help to take on all the problems, accusing yourself of every single one of them.

Neither does it help to insist to yourself that you don't have any of them – as I said, this is not a blame game, it's a reality check.

Be realistic.

See what speaks to you, what points you see yourself in and to what degree.

You might be very risk adverse but never feel jealous or entitled.

You might lack self confidence but have great trust in the goodness of others (as long as it's not an unrealistic trust!)

Be honest with yourself, but also be kind to yourself.

You have to be able to see clearly before you can see to move forwards.

Think Big

Think Big

Big Thinking

Think Big

Start Thinking Big

There are many things in life that can create and maintain a habit of thinking small, but once you understand them you can begin to deal with them.

So now it's important to learn about thinking big.

It's amazing how it works. Positive, abundant thinking, along with action will help you create an abundant life that is the life of your dreams once you're not afraid to dream big and act big.

You Share Knowledge

Once you teach yourself to think big, you'll soon realize that sharing your knowledge isn't a scary proposition and that people aren't going to steal your idea and beat you at your own game.

Instead, you might discover that while a lot of people want to know about the topic, they don't want to do the work, they want you to prepare the information for them.

Look at the number of training courses there are for all sorts of subjects.

Training used to be about learning a new skill for work, or learning how to use a new computer program, as if learning a new skill was only about the workplace.

But now you can find training courses for all sorts of things, training courses always involve people sharing their knowledge.

For instance, you can find many training courses online, offered by people who are successful in their field.

Now you might think, why does anyone choose to teach other people the skills they use to make a living? Some people think this is a crazy idea.

Why would you teach other people how to do what you do? Why would you train your own competitors? Surely that would damage your business?

Well, it doesn't.

Some people will follow the course and use the knowledge they have gained to set up their

Think Big

own businesses, but everyone will bring their own character to it and be their own original.

People who offer these courses don't think in terms of scarcity.

Instead, they live their entire lives with abundance and it shows.

They are bigger than small ideas. They love the success that they have found and want to share it with others.

And you can find many examples, where people who have found success will share their knowledge so that other people can find success as well.

People who are big thinkers, who are successful in their field and who are open, grateful people love to share their knowledge. They want others to find the joy they have found, and they love it when someone else is a success as well. It makes the pie bigger, and everyone can have a share of the pie, that's how we all grow.

So take some time to think about what can you teach someone? You could teach a neighbour who admires your clothes how she can make her own as well. You could teach someone how to bake, how to use a computer, how to use their smartphone, how to save money by budgeting.

All of us have skills that we could share with others.

Could you take your skills out of your neighbourhood and into the world by going on-line. Just look at YouTube – look past the cat videos – and see how many people are sharing their knowledge with the world. All knowledge is valuable even if it's showing someone how to boil an egg. Everyone has to learn sometime.

So think about it and see how teaching your skills to others can add abundance to your life.

You Build Relationships

People, who aren't jealous, who don't think small and do not live their lives thinking there is only so much love to go around, tend to build relationships with others easily.

And they don't even worry about whether some people will like them or not.

They just don't care about that type of negativity.

They just open their heart and their arms to others easily, and regardless of what happens they know without a doubt that they will learn something from the experience.

Think Big

They don't do this in a needy, almost desperate way. It's not about wanting people to 'like' you. It's about being confident enough to be 'you'.

They know that you cannot make anyone like you, so if they don't like you really isn't your fault

The truth is that relationships are the cornerstone of our lives.

The more value you put into each relationship that you develop, the more people will gravitate toward you wanting to build a relationship with you.

More people will want to recommend you, help you, build you up, and know you.

Look around you and think of the people you know who are good at building relationships.

How do they do it?

Usually, they're positive people who aren't judgmental, jealous, or resentful. They are truly happy when someone else succeeds.

If you start thinking about how all your relationships are like a team, you can overcome a lot of relationship building issues. If you were on a baseball team and your teammate beat you on home runs for the year, would you be resentful or happy for them?

An abundant thinker, a big thinker would be happy for them and share information about how to improve their own performance – and if the teammate were also a big thinker, he would be happy to share. After all, it's a team and success makes them all successful.

You Love Your Competition

Competition is good.
Think about competition in business again.
When an industry has only one or very few competitors there isn't any competition and they become lazy.
There's no need to improve the product or the service, there is no need to work harder at being better, there's no need to compete for the customer.
When there is this kind of monopoly in an industry, the whole things stagnates and nobody wins.
But when there is competition everybody wins.
There is more positive thinking, there is more creative thinking, there's more of a drive to improve the product or service, to improve the customer service, to improve the range of services.

And the strange thing is, the more competition there is the more the market grows in most examples, so there is more for everyone.

The same is true personally.

When you have no competition, there is no drive to improve so you stagnate or even go backwards.

Think of relationships.

It's amazing how it can perk up your attitude to your partner if there's a little competition for their attention.

It's the same at work, competition for the top slot will give you the impetus to try harder, to meet your targets, to do well.

Competition is the lifeblood of a successful life. It doesn't have to be negative or secretive, the best competition is when you appreciate the skills of those around you and see your competition as the spur that makes you better.

You see it in sport all the time.

Sport is by its very nature, competition. But the competitors are also teammates. They travel together around the world, they practice together, they socialise together.

Of course they want to win, but their competitors are also their best friends, even siblings sometimes, and they spur each on to be the best that they can be, then they all reach greater successes than they would on their own.

So learn to love your competition rather than being fearful of it, whatever area of life you are competing in.

You Love giving.

When you are a big thinker, you don't restrict yourself to only giving what you think is expected of you.

In fact you positively enjoy giving more than is expected of you.

You don't dole out your time in small amounts, only giving the minimum you can get away with.

A big thinker enjoys being able to share their time and their skills to improve the lives of others.

The idea of karma is wonderful.

The more you give the more you get.

The world would be a much better place if more people believed in karma, if more people were big thinkers.

If you only give you feel when you feel you have to, you will feel resentful of giving anything.

But when you change that mindset to giving because you want to, and giving more than is expected of you, and giving from the pleasure of giving rather than because you expect to receive - you can relax.

You can enjoy the joy you give to others, you can stop keeping a mental spreadsheet of what you get in response to what you give.

Giving freely can open up some incredible doors for you, opportunities that you would never have imagined can be there for you, simply because you were generous enough to give more than expected.

You're Optimistic

Once you let go of thinking small and embrace thinking big, dreaming of your future and building your big dream will feel wonderful.

You will be able to look into the future with optimism. You will be able to plan your dreams and make them reality.

Another saying for you;

'a dream without a plan is just a dream, a dream with a plan is a goal'

And of course a goal needs a plan of action to make it achievable.

So, if you want to write that novel instead of thinking of all the reasons you can't. (I don't have time. The baby won't let me. I can't work when they're sleeping.) You'll think of ways to do it.

Write for one hour after the kids go to bed.

Write for one hour in the morning before they get up.

Hire someone to help you with the family or to do another chore that takes up your time and prevents you from writing.

Cut down on your socialising or reduce the time in front of the TV or on the computer or iPad.

You can and should make a plan for anything you want to achieve.

Actually start that training to improve your career. Don't just tell yourself it will take four years. If you don't start it now, where will you be in four years? What will you have done with that time and money that you didn't spend on training?

If you want a special dream holiday, dream home, dream wedding – the dream that is financially out of reach – start a saving plan.

Will you miss the coffee each morning on the way to work, will you miss a takeaway. Let me assure you, when you begin to see the savings account begin to build, you will willingly give up some of that unnecessary spending.

Optimism is contagious. It creates positive forward-motion that brings results and this helps to continue the cycle.

So take control and make your plan.

You Take Risks

Being risk positive isn't really the opposite of risk aversion.

It simply means that you study the situation so that you can make good choices about the risks that you take.

So, if you want to make money online, you study how other people make money online, you study the product or service, you do some market research, then you take direct action toward that goal without worrying about what could go wrong.

It doesn't mean you jump out of an airplane without a parachute on that charity jump. That's just silly.

It means that you ensure that your parachute is ready for you to jump. That your jump partner is experienced and an expert. You accomplish this by creating detailed plans that you study and test to be reassured that your actions will more than likely lead to success.

Think Big

It's the difference between investing your money in a diverse way and investing it all with one bank or one person.

Both have some risk, but diverse investing always has less risk – not putting all your eggs in one basket is always a good plan.

Once you have the knowledge and the information that you need and once you believe in the action you are going to take, a risk that might seem incredibly foolish to other people, is actually well balanced to you.

That's the difference between entrepreneurs and those who stay in a 9-5.

There's absolutely nothing with the security of a 9-5, most people want to work to live rather than live to work, a steady wage is exactly what most people want, it gives them time and money to do things they really want to do with their lives outside work.

The problem is with the folk who are not happy with that, who constantly think they want to be free to run their own lives, be their own boss, set their own timetable – but never risk making the jump.

That just makes them unhappy, bitter, dissatisfied.

If you really, truly, deeply want something – you have to make the leap. You have to take the risk.

And that can be in any area of life.

A new job, an entirely new career, a new home, a new relationship – even a new hairstyle or a new look.

If you really – deep down want to do something, you have to take the risk.

So believe in yourself and your goals and your plans. That is the way to achieve success

You Are Grateful

As you begin to experience success, it's important to feel grateful instead of afraid.

Fear is a limiting belief and it can paralyse you and stop you taking any action to improve your life.

The more you give in to fear the worse it gets until the walls of your world close in and can suffocate you.

On the other hand, being grateful is an abundant emotion.

The fact is, the more grateful you are about your life the more you'll work to ensure that you have the life that you dream about having.

Think Big

Being grateful is a very positive emotion, it opens you up, it makes you relax, you can physically feel the tension lift from your shoulders as if a weight is being lifted off you.

It means that you are open to seeing new ideas and new paths in life.

It's also very attractive.

It will draw other people to you which in turn will give you more opportunities to succeed and be happy.

It can seem odd at first but like all habits, practice makes perfect.

Start off each day by thinking of three things you are grateful for.

- That the sun is shining.
- That it's raining – the garden needs rain.
- That you were able to have breakfast.
- That someone smiled at you.
- That you finished a piece of work.
- That you spent time with friends
- That you spent time with loved ones.

It doesn't matter what you're grateful for, it doesn't have to be something huge and life changing and the more you notice the small things in life the easier and more satisfying the practice of gratitude will become.

It's also a good idea to finish each day by reminding yourself of things that have happened during the day and being grateful for them.

It's a much more positive way to end the day than focusing on things that went wrong or things you could have done differently.

Be kind to yourself and look on the bright side of life.

You are Confident

A lot of people find it difficult to feel confident about their abilities, but big thinkers do believe in themselves.

Confidence isn't the same as arrogance.

In fact a lot of people who come across as arrogant aren't really confident, it's almost as if they are trying to compensate for their lack of self confidence by trying to convince everyone else - and themselves - that they do know what they're doing.

Confidence is a matter of believing in your own abilities and not feeling the need to prove it.

It's about knowing that you are good enough and capable enough in what you do.

Confidence can be built both through success and failure, as long as you learn the lessons that each will bring.

Some of the most successful people in the world have failed along the way.

The difference is that they have known how to pick themselves up and dust themselves off, learn the lessons and try again.

As Thomas Edison said, "I have not failed, I have just found 10,000 ways that do not work".

Think Big

Put the plan into action

Think Big

Think Big

How to Succeed

'There's nothing either good or bad but thinking makes it so.'
Hamlet, Shakespeare

Now that we have taken a look at the different aspects of thinking small or thinking big, and the way it can impact on your entire life, it's time to look at areas of life that this whole attitude can affect.

The way you approach any part of your life, will control whether you are able to be happy in life or not.

Whether you are able to reach your goals or whether you will never be quite successful enough.

Your attitude will colour everything, your relationships, your career and prosperity, your mental health and your physical health, even your family health.

The way you look at life will direct your life.

If you think about it you will have seen examples of this.

You may know two people who have been affected by the same problems, health problems, career problems, money problems or relationship problems.

But the outcome will have been totally different for each one.

One of them will have been crushed by the problem, they will collapse under the weight of their tragedy and it will define the rest of their lives. They will have been depressed, defeated and demoralised.

The other will have taken the same problem, the same set of circumstances, the same devastating effect and will have risen above it.

They will have found a way through the problem, a way to make the most of the hand they have been dealt no matter how bad it has been.

Now this is not to say that the problem is insignificant, it could have been life changing, but whether you are destroyed by it or you find a way through it is entirely up to you.

It's the way you look at it.

Think Big

Whether the glass is half empty or half full.

Whether the cloud has a silver lining or it's just a never-ending thunderstorm.

A life changing accident will utterly destroy one person while another person will go on to become a Paralympic athlete.

A financial disaster will send one person into a total decline while it will spur another onto massive success.

This is not the same as saying it's your own fault when things go wrong, the blame game never helps in any situation.

I absolutely don't mean that people deserve what they get – most people don't deserve it at all.

But the fact is that things happen, and you can never change the past, only learn from it and make the most of the future.

And the way you approach the problem will determine the effect it will have on the rest of your life.

No matter what life might throw at you, after you have dealt with the initial devastation and the time has come to move on, thinking small will make it worse while thinking big will allow you to make the most of the cards you have been dealt and of whatever opportunities come your way.

Personal Life

We all have a lot going on in life.

There's work, career, school, friends, home and family.

The list goes on and on.

In fact sometimes it can seem endless, and endlessly focused on someone other than you.

It's so easy to lose sight of what your personal goals are.

And I do mean your personal goals, the things that at the end of the day will make you happy, that will make your life better.

- You might want to finish a degree,
- you might want to complete a training course,
- you might want to retrain entirely
- you might want to strike out on your own
- you might want to relocate
- you might want to get fit
- you might want to take charge of your health
- you might want to write a book
- you might want to perfect or learn a hobby or new skill.

Think Big

You have all these plans, all these wishes but you don't actually get around to any of them.

You say that you don't have the time, but in fact the truth is that you don't make the time.

When you think about it, when someone else wants you to do something, somehow you find the time.

So why do you never find the time for your own dreams?

Everyone has time they don't use affectively.

Could you take an hour away from the TV and invest it in yourself?

Could you cut that coffee morning that you don't really enjoy and spend the time on yourself instead?

Does your job make financial sense, or do you spend more on travel, childcare and convenience meals than you earn?

Your time is valuable and it's the only thing that we can't get more of, so spend yours wisely.

The problem is it's too easy to bounce around achieving nothing, so you need a plan.

Creating, and following, a plan is essential for success.

There's that old saying again, fail to plan and you plan to fail.

So where should you start your planning?

Think Big

Choose one goal at a time – it's far too easy to get overzealous when looking at our personal goals.

New Year's resolutions are a very good example of this.

It's the New Year and you want to change your entire life all at once.

You decide you want to lose weight and improve your fitness, you want to clean out clutter, you want to take a class, earn a certificate, learn a new skill - all at the same time.

Naturally that is never going to work, so you spiral out of control and fail on all of them.

Worse than this, you stop trying because you climbed too high, too fast and fell far too short of your goals, leaving you thinking that there is no point in trying in the first place.

But that is not true.

It's just the way you went about it that is the problem.

Thinking big doesn't mean trying to do everything at the same time, thinking big is about being positive and focused.

So start with one goal at a time.

Focus on one thing and direct your energy into that.

Think Big

Allow yourself to take the time to succeed and allow yourself to appreciate each successful step along the way.

Congratulate yourself, give yourself a pat on the back, you can even reward yourself as you reach each target.

That will give you the enthusiasm and the feeling of success that you need to go on to hit the next target. Take everything in bite-size chunks and before you know where you are you will have reached the big target. You will have succeeded.

Picking a series of steps makes any goal much easier to achieve.

Whatever you are tackling, whether it's revision, losing weight or transforming your life, if you look at the whole picture at one go it can seem overwhelming leading you to giving up before you even tried.

But if you break it down into small steps, each one is achievable, and each time you achieve it you will have a feeling of success that will bolster you and give you the inspiration to take on the next chunk.

This means that you will keep positive and driven throughout.

You will build your confidence and your belief in yourself and you will find that thinking big is a much better way to run your life. It will lead to happiness.

Your Career

Career goals are important in everybody's life and they're certainly important if you want to work towards a successful life, whatever your career is.

Career goals can be a bit easier to identify, after all not all of them are set by you.

You may have a promotional system at the company you work for. They may have training programs in place for those who want to advance. This makes it much easier to choose your gaols because you don't have to decide on what they are and the path you need yourself

If you are running your own business, you will have an idea of what you want to achieve, how you want your business to grow, what you want to get out of it in the medium or long-term.

So you start the process in your career with a map already for you to follow.

Before you can decide where you want to go you have to know where you are starting from, so taking the time to examine where you are at the moment is a very useful process.

Examine and explore which area of your career or business is not working.

Think Big

Ask yourself what your end goal is – do you want to retire earlier, work fewer hours, or have more power? What really is your end goal?

And I do mean 'your' end goal, not just what you think it should be or accept as the norm. it's your life, so you should set your own goals.

Once you have discovered your end goal, start creating a plan of action.

Pick five action steps, beginning with the smallest.

Write them down. If you've read any of my other books, you'll have noticed by now that I'm a huge fan of actually writing things on paper. When it's written on a piece of paper it is much more 'real' than simply having it as a note on your smart phone or tablet.

There is still a lot to be said for physical reminders.

Once you have your step-by-step plan, take one small action step per day for a set amount of time – for example, three weeks.

This is an achievable goal rather than an overwhelming task, a bite-size piece of your plan that is easier to digestive.

Once you have achieved this first step it will get you closer to the second action step.

You may want start work earlier or make sure that you are on time for three weeks. Turning up

Think Big

at work on time is always going to improve your career opportunities.

You might decide that want to speak up at meetings rather than sitting quietly in the background, make your voice heard, make people notice you. Being invisible is never good for promotion.

You may want complete a training programme which will put you in line for a pay rise or a promotion.

You may want to take on more responsibility at work to show your new boss what you are capable of.

As with all goalsetting, breaking the process down into bite-size chunks makes it much more achievable because each step is small enough to be dealt with rather than allowing the whole task to overwhelm you.

So decide what your aim is, what your goals should actually be, where you want to get to at the end of the process.

If you decide you want to work somewhere else you might need to update your training and skills, you'll need to update your CV or resume, you'll also need to spend some time working out what you want and what you should apply for. Each step gets you closer to your goal.

Setting goals

Goals aren't just for work.

A good plan and a clear goal can help you achieve in all areas of life.

Or it might be something closer to home – even in the home.

If a new kitchen is your goal but it just seems too big a task to contemplate, break it down into a plan. Find out what you could have, find out what it would cost, work out what you can afford, what you need and when you could actually achieve your plan. Is it worth taking the plunge now or waiting a year to save up the money to get what you really want?

It's the same if you want to plan your wedding.

What do you want?

How long are you prepared to wait?

Do you want something small and romantic? Then maybe you should decide to resist the pressure to plan a lavish, expensive event.

Deciding what it is you really want can help with anything. It can get you to the future that you actually want rather than leave you drifting, tossed around by ideas from other people and the tides of life

Think Big

Once you know where you want to get to, you can design your roadmap, your action steps and once you have that, you can start your journey.

It might sound simple, and that's because really it is. You have no chance of achieving success if you don't know what success you are aiming for. You wouldn't start out on any journey without having a destination in mind.

Your relationships

The whole point of this book is to help you to learn to think big, to aim for your dreams, to be successful, and it's important to have that success throughout your life.

It's not enough to be successful in your career or financially, to be happy in life, to feel that you have succeeded, you need to be successful in all parts of your life.

Relationships are a huge part of anyone's life, and are the cornerstone stone to a truly happy, successful life.

When I talk of relationships, I don't only mean romantic relationships although of course they are a huge part of someone's life. But I am talking about all sorts of relationships that make your life worth living.

Think Big

Your relationship with your family, your parents, your siblings.

Your relationship with your friend's, with your work colleagues and people you mix with socially.

Relationships can also extend to the way you interact with your neighbours, the way you react to people on the street, or people in the queue at the store.

If you expect the worst from other people it will show in your attitude, and you will probably receive poor treatment.

But if you expect the best, if you are prepared to be open, if you are prepared to smile and help other people, they are much more likely to react positively to you and life will be better for everyone.

It's become almost acceptable to rage at other people, whether that is road rage, shop rage, or raining insults on social media, but it doesn't do anybody any good.

Not the person on the receiving end and not the person lashing out with outrage.

It's small, petty and bitter.

It will make you unhappy, angry and give you an ulcer!

Think Big

On the other hand, thinking big, being positive can improve any relationship in your life, no matter how fleeting.

And of course it's more important when you use these skills with the really important relationships in your life.

A successful relationship means being honest with yourself, being honest about who you are and how you come across to other people.

When you think big and are positive about life, you can accept the part that you play in life.

Far too many people choose the route of blaming everyone else for the things that go wrong rather than taking responsibility for their part, but the result is that they tend to become bitter, defensive and basically unhappy.

So learn how to be honest with yourself. After all is really no point in lying to yourself.

Take a look at how your actions your thoughts and your ideas will affect other people.

See if you like yourself.

The thing is if you don't like yourself why should you expect anybody else to like you?

So if you want to have a successful and happy life it's really important to be a person you would like to spend time with

The blame game never really works, it might help you score points but will never achieve anything at the end of the day.

In business, when a boss or CEO blames their employee, their employee becomes defensive and less cooperative, the customers just feel angry and devalued, the business does not do well.

But when a CEO guides and leads by example and makes reasonable requests for change and prosperity, people will follow suit.

When a company accepts responsibility for a mistake they have made, the customers will feel that is a genuine partnership and will become a loyal customer for the future because they have been treated well and their opinion has been valued.

If you make a complaint about a meal in a restaurant and they are negative about it you will never go there again, you will tell your friends and they won't go, and you'll tweet or Facebook about it and lots of people you've never heard of will decide not to go.

But if they treat you well, apologise and make amends, you'll use all those pathways to praise them – everyone wins.

This is the true meaning of a successful relationship, and the principle is true for any relationship.

Money

Money can be at the centre of many of our problems.

We can feel guilty about wanting more.

We can feel that we are being greedy because we want more.

We can feel that we don't deserve it, we can feel that we don't have enough of it, we can feel jealous because we don't have more.

It can colour everything.

"Money is the root of all evil."

The fact that this often quoted cliché is actually misquoted, goes a long way to explaining our problems with money.

The quote from the Bible is actually,

"the love of money is the root of all evil".

And those three little words, *"the love of"*, make all the difference.

Money is not evil.

Wanting sufficient money and more money than you have is not evil.

Think Big

We live in a financial world, everyone needs a certain amount of money to survive in the modern world.

We need to be able to pay our taxes, afford insurance, buy food and clothes and have a social life.

Even if you're self-sufficient you need a certain amount of money.

So money does not automatically equal greed and there is no shame in having more money as one of your targets.

At the same time you don't want to allow money to control you. It should be your servant not your master.

That's where the 'love of money' can come in. if you chase money for it's own sake you will have lost sight of the bigger picture, the path to happiness and success.

Unlike the ideas of the 1980's – greed really isn't good, because if you think like that there will never be enough to meet your idea of success.

So take a little time here to think about your attitude to money and what role it plays in your idea of success.

What is your money story?

We all have stories around money and it's important to uncover your own story.

Think Big

Do you believe you're not good enough to make the kind of money you dream of or do you believe only greedy people have and receive money? Do you believe that if one person has it, another person loses – there's only a certain amount to be shared out?

Once you uncover your negative attitudes to money and how you are sabotaging yourself with your money habits, you can begin to write your new story.

Start practicing positive affirmations around money.

- More money can flow easily into my life and for positive reasons.
- I can create abundance.
- I feel excited and positive about the abundance of money flowing into my life.
- Financial prosperity is possible in my life.

Practice these positive affirmations daily, in fact several times a day, visualize your bank balance showing larger numbers and imagine your life with financial abundance.

Positive affirmations can have amazing effects in all areas of life.

You are re-wiring your brain to be more positive and more open. This means that you are removing the mental blocks that stop you succeeding.

It may be a bit strange at first, but you have to overcome a lifetime of negative messages, so persevere, believe in the power of your positive affirmations and you will find that you are creating a new reality for yourself.

Life Purpose

Finding your life purpose, realising what you are supposed to be and to achieve in your life can be truly transformative.

All of us have a life purpose, but many of us never really discover what it is.

We end up living someone else's life, the life that other people think we should have, the life that we have been programmed to expect and accept.

The sad fact is that is never going to lead to happiness and success.

How can you win when you're running someone else's race?

It can be a difficult habit to break, this living somebody else's plan, but it is vitally important. No one wants to get to old age and realise that they never achieved anything that they really dreamt of.

Think Big

To paraphrase another saying, it's better to have tried and failed, than never to have tried at all.

The problem is that it's all too easy to become comfortable in your dissatisfaction.

You always feel that there is something more that you want to be doing, but your comfort zone is almost like a paralysing drug, it's very difficult to push yourself out of that, to take the risk, to reach into the unknown, to risk success.

It's too easy to make excuses and to stay where you are even if that is unsatisfying. It's a known dissatisfaction, rather than an unknown and untested possibility of success.

So you use excuses to hold yourself back from finding your true life's purpose.

You're too busy, you don't have the time, you can't take the financial risk, you're not old enough, you're too old.

You'll do it tomorrow, next week, sometime, never.

But if you truly want to find success and happiness and pursue your life's purpose and goals you have to make some changes.

You have to get out there and do it.

Get out of your head and into your heart. Sometimes we just analyse things too much, we spend too much time thinking instead of doing.

But if you want to succeed you need to move those ideas from your head to your heart, you need to feel them deeply and then take action

Take time to be quiet and sit still. Whether you go to the beach, the countryside or the park, you need to schedule time in to be quiet. As odd as it may sound, scheduling time to be quiet will actually help you to get into the process of being quiet anywhere, anytime randomly.

When you sit still and get quiet, you can actually hear a little better than you normally do when there is so much noise in your head. You can hear the birds, the wind in the trees, the waves crashing on the beach, you can also hear your own thoughts

Take notes, you know my love of pen on paper. Take time to journal your thoughts and feelings on paper. When you journal, when you write with pen on paper, you stop worrying about filters. You don't have to worry about what people will say, respond or how they think.

So get the pen and notepad out and write down your private thoughts, dreams, desires and wishes for your life purpose. Paper is more real than a computer screen or tablet. There are good reasons why so many people are returning to the old-fashioned pleasure of a journal.

Think Big

Learning the practice of being quiet will teach you how to clear your mind of the clutter of everyday life. Will be able to see your goals clearly.

When you read your notes, you will get a clear vision of what your goals are, and then you can act on them

Make a declaration to yourself.

You will reach your goals.

Once you can see clearly you can begin the process of declaring your life purpose.

Make positive and happy statements about how excited you are about pursuing your life purpose.

Keep it simple, don't elaborate and allow people to ask their questions or give their negative responses. Don't allow them to deflate you or make you second guess yourself.

You don't have to have all the answers, you don't ever have to have all the questions.

The important thing is that when you don't have the answers, don't doubt yourself, just simply be open to finding the answers.

Keep declaring your passion and purpose and the answers will come in time.

Reaching Prosperity

Have you ever looked at somebody and wondered to yourself how they did it?

Lots of people feel the same way about others who are successful.

We tend to look at others and think they are lucky or they get all the breaks or their husband/wife/parent made it happen or they come from money. There's that money thing again!

It's human nature to make excuses.

Other people are successful, not through their own hard work and positive attitude, but because they had some unfair advantage. That makes it more acceptable that they have success and you don't.

But it's just an excuse, and it's the kind of excuse that perpetuates small thinking and stops you from creating your own success.

After all, it was nothing they did, it was just handed to them on a plate, and if it hasn't been handed to you on a plate then obviously you can't get there.

Well it's true, that attitude will not get you anywhere.

When it comes to prosperity, it is vital to understand that it's not a matter of waiting for prosperity and abundance to come to you. You create it.

Choose an area in your life where you want more prosperity.

Obviously prosperity covers all of life, but there will always be some area where your idea of or need for prosperity begins.

It could be in your career, your overall financial status, you might want to reduce or eliminate your credit card debt or increase your savings and improve your retirement fund.

Once you've focused on an area, take the following steps to create prosperity:

Prosperity is a mindset and once you understand that the rest will flow. Prosperity is not something that happens to you, it is something you make happen. So change your mindset around prosperity.

Your subconscious mind is responsible for your habits, even your prosperity habits. In order to tap into the power and leverage of the subconscious mind, you will need to work on creating new mindset habits.

Take credit card debt, a big problem for a lot of people at the moment.

Focusing in on how much you owe, or burying your head in the sand and not even looking at the total isn't going to help you move forward.

Think Big

It also isn't going to help you if you give into the attitude that you are heavily in debt and there's nothing you can do about it.

And finally, there is absolutely no point at all blaming yourself about it and giving into a feeling of failure because you are in this position.

You can only ever start from where you are now,

You cannot change what happened yesterday, but you can accept where you are today and start planning on how to achieve a better tomorrow.

So take a clear look at your credit card debt and your income and create a plan.

There are books on budgeting that can help you with this, but the first stage is always to work out where you are and believe that you can make a difference – a positive difference.

Considering the problem with a positive outlook rather than a negative one is the only way you can actually solve any problem.

When you think big, you will think positive. You won't beat yourself up for past mistakes or consider that the situation you find yourself in is impossible to solve. You will look for the answers, look for the steps you can take and then follow that plan.

Think Big

So for instance if you are dealing with debt, the first step is to work out exactly how much the debt is.

Then look at your spending, most people have no idea what they spend, so it is a good idea to keep a money diary for at least a week, preferably a month.

It will surprise and probably horrify you how much money is frittered away on things that you can't even remember having, whether that is a coffee on the way to work, a magazine that doesn't get read, or a cake that you don't need. When you add up all these small amounts you can begin to take charge of your finances, and begin to work towards creating your prosperity.

Once you know what your money picture actually is, you can make a plan towards clearing debts, getting rid of the most expensive ones first and working onwards to the rest of them.

They you can look at your larger bills and work out a plan for controlling them and reducing them? Do you really need the full cable package? Do you ever use the gym membership?

The finish line might be in the distance, but at least you now have a finish line, you are working towards achieving a better tomorrow.

Having and acting on this plan will also make you feel better today. It will make you feel more

Think Big

prosperous, instead of worrying about the debt you will be able to focus on your goal of paying it off.

The very fact that you are doing something positive about it will make you feel more in control, you will be reprogramming your subconscious, you will feel more positive, that you can take action and you can improve your life.

In a more general way, prosperity isn't anything to do with an actual figure in your bank account.

There are millionaires who are always on the brink of disaster, while there are others who always feel that everything will be wonderful once they reach their first million and endlessly put happiness off, waiting for that magic moment.

But true prosperity is really having a personal feeling of abundance.

So you need to discover that your personal abundance is.

One person will feel poor because they can't have the latest Chanel or Hermes handbag, another will be delighted with the bag they have or a new one from the local artists market.

Think Big

Having a happy and successful life is about your own personal abundance rather than a constant quest to keep up with others.

You need to be able to stop chasing the dreams that others have set for you and work on your own dreams instead.

Abundance isn't a figure in a bank balance, it's a personal feeling inside you.

Think Big

Achieving success

Think Big

Learn how to Achieve your goals

We've looked at how important it is to have goals.

At the whole idea

At the fact that without having goals you're just a dreamer.

Goals are the things that help you turn daydreams into reality.

But it's important to have a method of being able to achieve your goals time after time.

Once you have a method that works for you, achieving your goals and achieving happiness and success is just a matter of following a plan that you understand.

So what is that method?

Have Action steps

No goal is achieved without this first important step.

It is vital you get out of your dreams and into your reality and then into action. Without small, measurable action steps, your success remains nothing but a story.

Break it into small steps and bite size pieces and start on building your future.

It is important not to get over zealous with your goals and do not take on too many at the same time.

Stick with one goal or one set of actionable and measurable goals.

When you use this method and set yourself new goals, new plans and new action steps you will be able to look back over the month or the year and see the path you have taken and how much you have achieved.

That will give you a great sense of satisfaction and give you the drive to take the next set of steps.

As they say, success breeds success, and whoever 'they' are, they're right.

Hold yourself accountable

Once you've set your goals and your bite-size pieces, you cannot just set that aside and ignore it. You have to check-in with yourself every once in a while.

Make sure that you're keeping on track with the plan.

It's just too easy to plan the plan and then think you've done what you need.

You haven't.

That's like buying a book and leaving it on the shelf. Buying it is not enough – you need to take it off the shelf and read it.

Until you put your plan into action – and keep it in action – it's still just a dream.

So keep track of yourself and your action.

Make certain you ask yourself the hard questions and tell yourself the truth about why you didn't do something.

After all, no point making excuses to yourself.

If you do find that you're slipping off the plan, don't beat yourself up about it just make sure that you get back on track.

Every day is a new start, so you didn't quite keep to the plan yesterday or last week, today you can start again.

The important thing is not to give up. Just because you had a chocolate bar yesterday doesn't mean you have to have another today.

Just because you spent more than your budget last week doesn't mean should go on a shopping spree today.

Just because you didn't write anything yesterday doesn't mean that you should give up on your idea of finishing your book.

Find the reason why, be honest with yourself and work out how to avoid the problem in the future.

You owe it to yourself to take your plan seriously.

Learn self-discipline.

If you want to succeed, if you want to reach your goals, if you want to learn how to be a positive thinker and a successful person, you need to learn self-discipline.

It's important to understand that anything in life takes practice.

No new skill comes fully formed on the first morning, so don't beat yourself up for the times that it doesn't work.

Just keep practicing.

You can take time off of course, life has to be enjoyable, but you need to keep to your plan for most of the time. Otherwise you will spend a lifetime of small rewards that are forgettable and meaningless, and never reach the real rewards of success and happiness. You have to focus on the big ideas, not allow yourself to get distracted by the small ideas and small thinking.

Like any skill, the more you practice the art of self-discipline, the more easily it will come to you and you will find that you get much more sense of satisfaction from knowing that you are sticking to the plan and are reaching your goals.

Talk to yourself

Now you might be saying at this point, what is she on about? I never talk to myself, it's a sign of madness!

You're telling yourself fibs again.

We all talk to ourselves, we all have a conversation going on in our heads.

The important thing is to make that sure that your inner voice is supporting you rather than undermining you.

Far too many people have an inner voice telling them constantly that they're not good enough, not clever enough, they don't deserve success, that this will never work.

And this holds them back throughout life.

It's difficult enough to overcome other people who are telling you you're not good enough, so why on earth should you tell yourself that you're not good enough.

You have to believe in yourself.

And why on earth shouldn't you?

So in order to achieve success in all areas of your life, it's very important to watch the self talk.

The better you talk to yourself, the better you'll feel and the more success and happiness you will experience in all areas of your life.

Picture it this way – would you talk to your best friend the way you speak to yourself sometimes? Would you accept the same messages that you give yourself from someone else?

No you wouldn't.

So accept that you do talk to yourself, accept that it is an important conversation, learn to be positive and encouraging.

Be kind to yourself.

Think Big

Checklist

Think Big

The Categories Of Life

Personal
- Choose one goal at a time – we all have the habit of getting overzealous in our personal goals and start out wanting to lose weight, diet and exercise, clean out clutter, take a class, earn a certificate, etc. And then, we spiral out of control and fail at all of the above.
- Begin to get excited, and it will show. Power tip – the more you get excited about what you are doing, the more inspired you will feel and the more momentum you will create.

Career
- Examine and explore which area of your career is not working.
- Ask yourself what your end goal is – do you want to retire earlier, work fewer

- hours, or have more power? What is your end goal?
- Once you have discovered your end goal, start creating a plan of action.
- Pick five action steps, beginning with the smallest.
- Take one small action step per day for a set amount of time.

Relationships
- Be honest about who you are.
- Take a look at your actions, thoughts, and pre-conceived notions when relating to others.
- Ask how you can show up as a contribution to the other person.

Money
- What's your story? We all have stories around money. It's your job to uncover your story.
- Once you uncover your negative money story and self-sabotaging habits surrounding money, you can now write your own brand new story.
- Start practicing positive affirmations around money.
- Practice these daily.

Life Purpose
- Stop Self-sabotaging behaviour.
- Practice leaving the comfort zone.
- Quiet your mind.
- Get_Clear.
- Make a Declaration to yourself.

Prosperity
- Choose an area in your life where you want more prosperity. Is it in your career, your financial status, credit card debt or savings and retirement?
- Positive thoughts create prosperity.
- Take on the practice of positive thinking.

For all of these categories, remember:
- Get quiet/get still.
- Write it down.
- Take action.
- Be accountable.
- Follow through.
- Celebrate smaller successes, which will lead to bigger ones.
- Keep up momentum with enthusiasm.

Momentum

Momentum is important to success, but how do you incorporate momentum into your daily life

Once you've got the skills, habits and mindsets in order, it's time to keep up the momentum.

The biggest mistake, when it comes to momentum, is that people start too big and fall short.

Allow enthusiasm and passion to fuel your drive rather than let all the action take responsibility for keeping up momentum. Nothing fuels momentum more than excitement.

But how do you incorporate momentum in your daily life so it doesn't overwhelm you?

Find something every day that leads towards your goal that makes you feel excited. When you are excited, you create your own energy.

Think Big

Create a plan – once you have the underlying feelings, you'll begin to notice momentum building up speed, however, you need to reign in that energy otherwise you might get overzealous. You may find yourself veering off into several other ideas and creative endeavours. Create a plan of action as to where that drive will carry you, so it doesn't carry you away.

It's really important to control your enthusiasm. Once you get started, ideas can fire up on all sides – that's a problem I have – but that makes it far too easy to get distracted and lose direction.

It's not that any of the ideas are bad, it's just that you'll never succeed when you try to do everything at once.

So build up your momentum on a single goal and focus.

They rest can wait until later. I keep notes that I can return to. If I write the idea down, I can park it. If I don't it just stays, cluttering up my mind.

Believe in yourself – above and beyond all things, belief in yourself is key.

Tune out the voices and opinions of others.

Failure is Your Best Friend

The fear of failure is actually much more damaging than failure itself.

It can be paralysing.

Like any fear, even the monster under the bed, the more you think about it the bigger and more powerful it gets until it strangles you and you are unable to function at all.

Fear is the mind killer.

A reasonable amount of fear is fine, it stops us doing stupid, dangerous things like walking along a crumbling cliff face and falling to our deaths on the rocks below.

But if that fear grows out of control and means that we won't go anywhere near a cliff face, not within a mile of one, not even standing on a slight rise, it becomes very limiting and just stops you living a full and enjoyable life. A successful and happy life.

Fear should be faced and then you will be able to see how small it really is.

Once you get over your biggest fear and actually experience it, you will see it's not the big elephant in the room you once though it was.

Failure is one of the biggest fears.

It stops people trying for something better than they have. It keeps people in small unsatisfactory lives.

Understand the definition of failure – failure is not taking action, not taking chances and not taking risks.

The fear of failure holds you back, not failure itself.

Failure shows you one of the ways that won't work and frees you to find another way that will work.

But failure can be a great force for success.

It shows you what doesn't work.

It makes you look at what caused the failure and how you can work around the problem.

It shows you the mistakes to avoid and each time you fail you will have learnt one more mistake not to make next time.

Failure is just another way of describing practice.

Think Big

You don't get things right first time, you have to learn, you have to practice, you have to be prepared to get it wrong, to fail and try again.

Otherwise none of us would every have learnt to walk or talk.

Every expert in every field has had to start from the beginning, and they will have made mistakes as they learnt, that's what practice is for.

Try, fail, learn, repeat – eventually you become an expert

The Reward System

Rewards are a great way of keeping you on track.

Even though you are moving towards your dream, you need to have some way of keeping up your energy on the journey and a reward system is a wonderful way of doing that.

But how do you create a reward system that works for you?

Well, the first thing is to create some system of keeping a record.

And you know my preferred way – keep a journal.

Keeping a journal is a perfect way of seeing where you have come from and how far you have come. It's not just a record of dry facts, it's a reminder of how you have felt at each stage, a reminder of the improvements, the successes and even the failures – as I said, you should learn from your failures.

So keep a journal, look at it as writing a letter to yourself, to your future self.
- every time you have a success write it down.
- every time you have a failure look at your journal and see exactly what you are made of and where you can change a habit.
- Whenever you reach a small goal, boast about it.

You can also keep yourself on track by involving others in your new life plan.

When you share your hopes and goals with someone else you are accountable. Someone else knows what your plan is and that makes it harder to just give up on it.

Making excuses to yourself is much easier than making excuses to others.

But make sure that you choose someone who will be supportive and don't share with people who will put you down or minimize your dreams and successes.

They will leach your energy and your drive towards a new positive attitude in life.

You don't need that toxic attitude in your life.

Allow yourself a treat every time you achieve a goal – it doesn't have to be big, but something

Think Big

that will make a connection in your brain and teaches you that achieving goals reaps rewards.

Rewards are a very good method of training for anyone and you should go with what works.

There's no point in making things harder than they have to be.

There's nothing intrinsically good about making your life difficult.

You want to be happy and successful, not persecuted and miserable.

How to Train Your Brain

In order to make serious changes in your life, you have to change the way you think about things

You have been working on your old world view all your life so you will have to accept that it will take some work to change and create a new world view for yourself.

To change from small thinking to big thinking.

You need to train your brain to have positive associations with things like money or work.

Choose which emotion you want to associate you plan for success with – is it fear of failure or is it joy, happiness and fulfilment?

Pay attention to your thoughts – you have the power of choice.

Don't let running on autopilot control your life.

Recreate your thoughts.

Retrain your brain.

Think Big

It might seem impossible, but you can change your thoughts at any time in life.

And it's important to change your thoughts from the negative ideas that you are so used to, maybe even comfortable with in a strange way, to more positive ones.

It's easy to dismiss the whole idea of using positive affirmations as some strange 'new age' idea and one of the first things you need to do is to change this particular mind set.

You are what you think.

As Shakespeare put into Hamlet's words, there is nothing good or bad but thinking makes it so.

You have accepted the negative affirmations that you and others have fed to you all your life;

- you're not good enough
- you're not pretty enough
- you're not clever enough
- you'll never get anywhere
- who do you think you are?

Its time to swap these vicious, negative messages for positive, joyful messages.

If you or someone else tells you something often enough, it becomes your reality, so it's time to start giving yourself positive messages.

It's all too easy to dismiss the whole idea of positive affirmations as some kind of mumbo-jumbo.

So I want to illustrate how real their power is and how transformative they can be by looking at the opposite.

For some reason, we seem to be much more willing to accept that something negative is true, rather than the opposite, positive effect.

Think of the child who was constantly told by parents, guardians, teachers, peers or even friends, that they are not good enough.

- You're lazy
- You're stupid.
- You're ugly.
- You're not one of us.
- You can't join our group, our team, our gang.

Such ugly words and phrases and they can cause terrible hurt and damage.

We've all seen it happen, to others if not to ourselves.

If you were on the receiving end, you know how the message can eat into you until you begin to believe it and that becomes how you see yourself.

I was lucky, I had very supportive parents who believed in me, and I was obstinate, so not very good at accepting some of the inevitable negative messages sent my way - everyone gets them at some point.

But I've seen other people slowly wither under the onslaught of negative messages, whether it happened to a child, in the workplace, in some social groups or later from a partner - someone who should support and love you but instead who damages and causes self-belief to wither.

Negative messages, negative affirmations, can wither the spirit, eat into the soul and destroy self-belief.

If negative messages can be so damaging and so effective, why should you dismiss the power of positive messages and affirmations?

Anything that you are told or that you tell yourself will become reality.

When you hear or repeat something often enough, it creates and then strengthens the neural links in your brain. It's how we learn, by repeating things, by practising, revising and strengthening those neural pathways.

So if you doubt the whole idea of positive affirmations, think again.

You may feel a bit strange, even a bit foolish at first but persevere. Be serious about it. Believe that it will work, don't doubt yourself, don't sabotage yourself by saying the words while believing it cannot work.

Do yourself a favour and believe in the power of your brain to transform your life.

Think Big

Find some positive affirmations that resonate with you and feel real to you and then repeat them several times a day until you re-wire your brain and it becomes your new reality.

The Art of Visualizing

If you allow yourself to focus on a problem for too long it has a habit of growing and growing until it becomes a monster that you just can't imagine being able to gain control over.

It really helps if you can visualise the problem and the way that you can overcome it.

Sometimes it helps to face it head on, to research the options and get on with it.

But there are times when it is better to take your mind off it for a while.

Concentrating on a problem without finding a resolution will just feed the problem. The more time you give it without coming up with a solution the more intractable it will become.

It will grow until it becomes that monster that you just cannot imagine yourself being able to defeat.

So come at it sideways.

Think Big

Have you ever looked for something and not been able to find it.

You search everywhere, turn the house or your office upside down. You might have managed to do some very overdue sorting out and tidying up – but you just cannot find the item you really need.

Then as soon as you give up in disgust and go and make a cup of coffee – there it is, smugly staring you in the face.

Taking a rest from trying to solve the problem works on the same principle.

Instead of focusing on the problem and sinking deeper and deeper into the impossibility of solving it, give yourself a rest.

Think of the good things about your plan, get enthusiastic about how excited you are about your dream and visualise how your life will be when your dream comes true.

Imagine your new life, focus on it until you can taste your success, really 'see' the details and name each stage, knowing it and making it real.

Think about the end result at this stage and not how you will get there. This way you will avoid the problem of creating monsters that you just don't need.

Think Big

Once you can really visualise how life will be it will take on a life of its own. It will become real, tangible, solid, achievable.

It's a matter of creating and taking the steps to get there, because the goal will no longer be just a daydream it will be the reality you just haven't arrived at - yet.

Meditate

Meditation is a wonderful tool.

Many of the most successful business people in the world include meditation in their daily routine.

So don't dismiss it as a another piece of 'new age' nonsense.

Many studies show that meditation can have real, physical affects on your health and well being

There are a number of different types of meditation and you should try different methods until you find a way that works for you, something that you feel comfortable with.

There are many books and courses to teach you meditation and it's certainly too big a subject to deal with in a few pages here, so all I'm going to do is try and open your mind to the idea of meditation.

Think Big

It doesn't really matter if you call it meditation or prefer to follow the idea of mindfulness, what you want to do is take yourself out of the chaos of your mind. Away from the busy mind that gets distracted by every little thing and into a calmer space where you will learn to slow down and quiet the mind.

Many people have the idea that meditation means having a blank mind and think it's impossible for them because as soon as they try to think about 'nothing' their inner voices take off at high speed and deafen them.

But it's not about having a blank or empty mind, its about having a calm mind.

You can focus on your breathing.

You can focus on a sound.

You can focus on a prayer.

You can focus on a positive affirmation.

You can focus on adult colouring.

You can focus on anything that will work for you and help you to calm your mind.

You can meditate at night, allowing you to reset your subconscious brain. Let the meditation play as you fall asleep, although meditation isn't about falling asleep!

You can meditate in the morning, beginning your day with a calm mind that will be much more effective in dealing with the rest of the day,

Think Big

allowing you to face the problems and challenges with a calm mind rather than in a caffeine fuelled panic.

Don't hold your breath.

When you're tense, you tend to hold your breath subconsciously.

Think about your breathing throughout the day.

Notice how tight your body is, especially your stomach and shoulders – let yourself relax.

Meditation is not wishy washy hippy stuff. It's a tool that the very successful use naturally in their everyday life.

So learn from those who have already reached their success and happiness.

"Half an hour's meditation each day is essential, except when you are busy. Then a full hour is needed." Saint Francis de Sales

Create Success Habits

In a large part, success is a habit.

Luckily, once success is a habit it can be self perpetuating.

True success in one part of life leads to success in the other parts of your life.

That is, of course, as long it is true success, the success that is real to you, your dream rather than just the sort of success that the outside world sees and judges you on, the success that you feel inside.

True success and happiness doesn't need the approval of anyone else.

So how do you go about fixing those success habits in your life?

Don't set unachievable goals

Create a pathway of small steps and one new habit at a time until that one is in place.

Think Big

Celebrate success both personally and with others.

Review your habits and see what hasn't worked as well as what has. Then you can refine your strategy for the next stage.

Make a decision. If it doesn't work simply make a new one – accept failure as a positive thing, a teaching aid.

Always be in action and in momentum, don't sit and analyse problems and plans for too long. Keep moving.

Delegate. Don't try and do everything yourself. Spend your time and energy on the things you are good at and delegate the things that are not your strength.

Learn how to say no. It's incredibly liberating and it becomes easier as you do it. People will also respect you more if you stop being a 'yes' person. When you start to think about your response before automatically saying yes, people will take your response – and you – more seriously

Give up the negative habit of procrastination, it's a time stealer and an energy stealer and it will make you feel worse and more negative over time, so don't give it any oxygen. Make a decision, act on it and then move on.

Think Big

Reward yourself for every goal achieved no matter how small, especially for the small ones.

Write it all down – yes, write it down, pen on paper not just notes on a screen, your success path in life is worth valuing and keeping for the future. Put your journal away and revisit it – you'd be surprised at how much you have achieved, and it will show you how far you have come, giving you the confidence and drive to continue on your success path.

And finally

It's called learning to think and aim big for a reason.

If you already knew how to put all these practices into place, then you wouldn't need any training.

And you most certainly can retrain your brain. It just takes practice.

The more you practice, the easier it will become. With these tips, practices, and goal-setting techniques, you'll be on your way to not only learning to think and aim big, but you'll be on your way to living big – a big, successful, happy life.

It will take effort – you are reversing the habits of a lifetime, but if you don't do it now – when?

Will you just continue to put your hopes and dreams on hold for the next year, the next ten years, the rest of your life.

As they – whoever they are – say, the longest journey starts with a single step and it's up to you when you take that first step.

In fact you have taken that first step – you've read this book to the end and I hope it has given you ideas that you can follow. That it has woken you up to what is holding you back and what you can do to change that.

It's a short book rather than a door stop because I want it to spark ideas and make you take action rather than get bogged down in the detail.

At the end of the day, you are the only one who can answer the important questions.

What do you want in life?

Why do you want it?

What do you expect it to feel like once you get there?

What are you prepared to do to reach your goals?

Are you worth chasing your dreams?

The answer to that last one is easy;

Yes You Are

Enjoy the journey.

More books by Josie Baxter:

How to Set your Personal Boundaries: Learn to say No and Protect yourself from Overwhelming Stress

Magic Mornings: How a good morning routine can transform your entire life

How to be Happy: 101 Ways to Improve your Life

Resolve to Succeed: How to crack the New Year's Resolution

Printed in Great Britain
by Amazon